ExtraOrdinary

The Extraordinary Life of
Louise Blake

Blake Roberts

ISBN: 979-8-218-53760-9
First Printing October 2024

Cover Design & Interior Layout:
Jessica Tilles of TWA Solutions & Services

Printed in the United States of America

Table of Contents

From the Author...

When I tell people I'm the youngest of seventeen children, the question that always follows is, "By the same mother and father?" The short answer is "No," but that response never quite captures the truth. The reality is far more complicated than biology. I've never thought of my siblings as "half," and Mom never considered her children as anything but her own—no halves, no steps. In our family, love and commitment always took precedence over DNA. Blood may define us biologically, but love, family, and the bonds we build together are what truly make us whole.

Years after Mom and Dad were married, she attended a celebration at my brother Bemis' home. Mae Liza, Dad's first wife and Bemis' birth mother, was also there. It was the first time Mom and Mae Liza had seen each other in over forty years. They greeted each other with a hug and a kiss on the cheek as if they were old friends. Mom said they talked for a while about the children—not "her" children or "Mom's" children, but simply the children. It surprised Mom that Mae Liza knew all of her children's names, having heard so much about them.

In the community where I grew up, the bonds between us ran deeper than the DNA in our veins—they were about ownership and responsibility to one another. The shared Black experience in America was, and still is, thicker than blood. One home was everyone's home, one child was everyone's child, and one parent was everyone's parent. If you misbehaved in the streets, someone might give you a whooping on the spot, and then you could get another one when you got home. Instead, there was a sense of safety and common purpose in who you knew—and who knew you.

This sense of community extended beyond our streets and neighborhoods, reaching some of the White members of our community as well. In the 1960s, South Bend, Indiana, was a hotspot for tornadoes. One afternoon, just as an elementary school let out, a freak tornado touched down while children were trying to make their way home. The owner of the only White-owned auto shop threw open his big garage door, ushering all the children inside to safety before notifying their parents.

Some of these things I speak of, I remember from when I was a child, while others are memories etched into my soul, shaped by the stories Mom, Dad, and my siblings have shared over the years.

For Mom, like many people of color living in America, survival depended on navigating hurdles, avoiding pitfalls and injustices, and escaping the threat of lynchings, all while striving to live extraordinary lives.

I have no "steps" in my life, only shoulders that I stand on, shoulders that have all uniquely given me love, nurturing, safety, and the wisdom to know the difference.

It's with profound gratitude that I give thanks and honor to:

God first...

My parents: Hartie Blake and Louise Owens Blake

Varnia, Bemis, Louise, Emma, Creasie, Bernice, Gladys, Bessie, Hardie Jr., David, Fred, Dorine, Sharon, Jessie, Forestine, and Walter—the shoulders I stand on.

Louise Blake

Preface

I first got the idea to write this book back in 2007. I was brimming with enthusiasm and couldn't wait to dive in, and Mom's excitement matched mine. We both looked forward to our daily conversations as we reminisced about her memories from early childhood to the present day. I asked her questions and made notes as she shared her stories. This entire experience of talking with her to write a book about her was new and exciting for both of us.

Putting precise years and dates on the times and events proved quite challenging. However, the stories were fluid, colorful, and heartfelt. Many of the things she told me about growing up in the South were heartbreaking, but with decades

1

separating her from the pain and hurt, she could tell her stories with a touch of humor.

As we unraveled her life, I appreciated the extraordinary lives she and millions of women of color must have lived. Her stories were our stories—tales of Black ancestors torn from their native Africa and enslaved. It helped me understand the migration of Black people from the South to the North. I wondered how those who remained in the South endured. Life, death, and misery were all interwoven into the fabric of her narratives. Death wasn't always the end, and I found the discussions about "haints" captivating. In the past, haints were a common term used to refer to ghosts and they were more prevalent and widely accepted. I imagined tormented and restless souls unable to rest in peace because of the suffering they endured in life.

Days turned into weeks, weeks into months, and months into years, and slowly, memories started fading and becoming harder for Mom to access. I witnessed the gradual toll aging takes on all of us. It was disappointing that I hadn't finished the book in weeks or months, as I had intended. I avoided finishing because I dreaded what the final chapters might not look like. I wanted my story's strong, triumphant matriarch to remain as she was in the beginning. However, I could see her becoming frailer and more fragile with each passing day. I feared how many more chapters I would have to tell. Trying to write a book about an extraordinary life while facing my mom's mortality became even more challenging as I came face to face with my mortality. Life can be a real bitch sometimes.

In 2011, I was diagnosed with cancer. My battle with it marked a new chapter in both of our lives. My first thought was that she would be my go-to for strength and encouragement, no matter what the situation was.

This took me back to a time when I mustered the courage to tell her I was gay. I was in college, and we were in the middle of one of our many telephone conversations when I just blurted out, "You know I'm gay, right?"

She responded, "Yes."

The conversation then went from "Did you know?" to "When did you know?"

Without hesitation, she replied, "I'm sure I knew long before you did."

That opened up a whole new discussion. I then asked why she said nothing about it. She told me she thought when I was ready to talk about it, I would.

Then came the big question. I asked her if it bothered her or if she had a problem with my being gay.

In her usual calm and matter-of-fact way, she said, "I couldn't love you any more or any less." Then she added, "And I didn't feel like I had a choice."

"Why?"

"Because I knew if I didn't accept it, you would have said 'to hell with me' and been gone from our lives," she explained.

"Your dad and I raised some very strong-willed children with their own minds and ways."

Just like that, it was out, over, and done. Before long, we were talking about something else.

I wondered if my mother would have a different reaction to the news of my cancer. Would it be a painful experience for her? With her declining health, vision, impairment, and occasional memory lapses, I questioned if she would still be the pillar of strength for me at that moment. Would she truly comprehend the significance of my cancer? Last, I pondered whether she would mourn the loss of her husband or her youngest child first. The answer came six months into my battle with cancer. In April 2012, she laid my father to rest. Although we may have discussed it, I have no recollection of ever speaking to her about my cancer again.

I was in the final stage of my treatment when I came home for my dad's funeral. Those days are just a blur to me now. What I remember most is that amid all the activities of planning our dad's service, Walter and I stayed close to Mom while the others managed the arrangements. While everyone else took care of things, Walter and I remained at the house with Mom.

I wasn't sure if it was mourning or something else, but I sensed she had begun a journey into a place inside herself that she might not return from. She would sit for long periods as we talked, without saying a word. Her eyes were closed, her expression stoic—lost and found all at the same time. There was no way of knowing what was going on in her mind, and it felt intrusive to ask. So, Walter and I made small talk with each other, making sure she knew we were there.

I felt like a child again, the one she would, on occasion, tell, "No, you can't come with me this time; you have to stay home with the others." I had never felt so close and yet so distant from her at the same time.

On the day of my dad's service, my sister Forestine, the youngest of the girls, said Mom had asked for Walter and me to ride in the funeral car with her. I don't know if it was because we had stayed so close to her over those few days, or if it was because we were her two youngest. At the gravesite, Mom stayed inside the car, and Walter and I stayed with her.

In 2019, twelve years after I started the book, she left us peacefully, surrounded by family at my sister Forestine and her husband's home. I felt like I had cheated her out of something important. She would never see her book come to fruition, but the zeal to tell her story reignited in me.

Looking back, I realized her story was too big for me to tell it all, despite the many reasons I had given for not finishing the book in the past. In my notes were stories that were profound, funny, and heartbreaking, and I wanted to share them. So, instead of writing a biography, I curated a collection of stories Mom told me and my siblings over the years.

Like so many other women of color, the strength, courage, and restraint that defined these women's lives—and my mother's life—is unmatched. I know firsthand the strength and restraint she had to muster with me over the years must have tested her many times. As her last child, and in her later years, I think I challenged her in ways that surpassed those of my siblings.

I must have been around eight or nine years old when, one day, Mom would not let me go outside because it was raining. I followed her every step, pouting and crying in her face the entire time. Even when she went into her bedroom, I trailed behind. I was a spoiled, chubby kid who wanted to go to the store for a Suzy-Q cake. She refused to give me money or let me go out in the rain.

A couple of hours later, when the rain stopped, she had had enough. She went into her purse, took out some money, and handed it to me. "Go get your coat and boots and go to the store before you make me kill you," she said.

I wasn't sure how to feel about that, but as long as I got my way, I figured I'd make peace with her later. I also remember Walter telling me, "You're gonna make her hurt you one day."

I will never forget that afternoon. It makes me laugh every time I think about it.

Marked for Death

You don't get a dress rehearsal for this life. Some believe in reincarnation which means you keep coming back until you get it right. I was raised with more traditional beliefs. The Bible might not have been the driving force in my upbringing, but my mother believed in basic principles. You might've heard me say it more than once that "the age of consent" was the most important. The age of consent in the Bible is the age at which a being becomes responsible for their own soul. I think the Bible places this at around twelve years old. Before that, the parent is responsible for the soul of the child. So, Momma kept us on the right path until we were off her tab. Later in life, I would do the same with my kids. I took them to church until they were old enough to decide for themselves if they wanted to attend or not.

That's just how you get started. We all come into the world and live the hand we're dealt. As a girl, I saw things, experienced things, and learned things right off the top that let me know you either set a path and take control of your life, or life will turn you every which way but loose. I never lived or knew any other place other than the South when I was a girl coming up, but I knew there must be something better than the South.

The South was even a tough place for some White folks. Just depends on what kind of White you were. What we called "poor White trash" was not treated any better than us. If it was tough for a White person, it was ten times as bad for us from all sides. There were a few places where poor White folks and Blacks got along pretty alright together. The poor Whites were treated like the rest of us by Whites with money, yet they thought that skin color made them better than us. That type ended up hating everybody. Those were the worst. Try as you may to get along with them, but you mostly find that there isn't a way to do that. We learned to live with them, just as we did with all White people. If only they learned how to live with us. Unfortunately, that's a lesson we still haven't learned all these years later.

I was born in a place called Marked Tree, Arkansas, in 1923, one of nine children. My mother's name was Lou

Creasie. Her maiden name was Patton. Her side of our family never knew what it was like to be a slave. They were straight from the Indian reservation. My mother's grandmother, Jenny Longstreet, was a full-blooded, Black Foot Indian. She took up with a Black man, and that was how we all came to be. My father was Dell Owens, and his grandfather was a slave. Of course, I never lived that experience, but had first knowledge of what life was like for slaves. My father was a direct descendant of former slaves. Just one generation removed from slavery, my father's father managed to get some land and started farming for himself.

> *We were called Black people back then, or*
> *at least that was the polite name they called us.*
> *Personally, for some reason, I never liked that*
> *term. Maybe because it was so close to "nigger" for*
> *me. My mother always taught us that a "nigger"*
> *was a low-down, good-for-nothing person. Then*
> *she would say, "And you're not low-down, or good*
> *for nothing, so you ain't a nigger."*

The South was about as miserable a place as a person could ever live. Another thing my mother would also say was "The only free thing in the South is a White man and a Black woman." It brought little comfort. I was just a girl, maybe six or so, when my father got into a scuffle with a White man.

9

Poppa said something the White man did not take too kindly to, and before Poppa knew what had happened, the White man hauled off and hit my father. When he raised his hand to hit Poppa a second time, Poppa caught him by the arm, wrenched it behind his back, and began beating the White man until he fell to the ground. Poppa stayed on him, beating him until some other men rushed over and pulled him off. He nearly killed the White man, and he would have had the others not stopped him. Some say Poppa did, in fact, kill him.

From the first blow, it made no difference if he would have killed the man or not, the outcome was the same for my father. Poppa was already marked for dead. There was no law that would see things from Poppa's point of view. By the time Poppa got home, everyone was speaking in hushed terms. Every noise outside put everyone on edge. There was no such thing as self-defense for a Black against a White man. If you raised your hand to a White man, you were automatically wrong, and the price you had to pay in most cases was unthinkable. The only option was to try to get out of town as quickly as possible. That, or more than likely my father would be jailed or dead before the sun came up the next morning. He would have to travel fast and light, which meant deserting his family. We didn't talk much about slavery or the past the way young people do today, we just got on with life and tried as best we could to make the best of it.

There were men and others who organized themselves in the church, but none of the things they did took place in the church, only the organizing part. They were the deacons, assistant pastors, and ushers who wore white gloves and hats with various symbols on them. Their members were kept a secret—no one knew and no one asked who they were. All you needed to know was they were the ones who came to you in situations like this.

Women folk played a limited role in these groups, too. The women often had to offer cover, feed, and hide men from time to time, without questions. Sometimes, it be for their own man and other times it might be for someone else's. They were responsible for my father getting out of town alive.

As a little girl, all I knew was that my father was in trouble, and everyone was nervous and upset. My mother went on with her typical doings and made me and my sisters and brothers go to bed, but we snuck and continued to watch whatever we could see. If Momma was afraid, she never showed it. She and Poppa whispered a lot and one or the other would occasionally look out the window like they were expecting someone. Momma packed some clothes and things, then she wrapped some bread, jam, and dried meats up and put them in a bag for poppa.

Then there was a knock at the door and Poppa slipped out the door into the dark. Momma began to clean and sweep the kitchen like she did any other night. Before long we all fell asleep until a little later at night when we were awakened by banging at the door like someone was trying to tear the house down.

We could hear Momma as she made her way to the door. She asked who it was and we could hear men shouting from the other side of the door. Momma opened the door and was confronted by several White men, asking for Poppa. I could hear Momma tell them that she had not seen him since early yesterday morning. She went as far as to say, "If you find him let me know."

One of the men, who identified himself as the sheriff, asked if she minded if they came in and searched the house. Momma told him, "Come right in, just please don't wake my youngins'."

The sheriff made a comment about Momma breast feeding White babies around town. I heard Momma ask him if he thought she was hiding my father in her breast. With that, the sheriff said he was sure that niggah was hiding somewhere in town, and they were going to find him.

Early the next morning, Momma woke us all up and had us all come out to the yard. Just a few minutes after we were all out in the yard, a wagon came down the road real slow as it passed our place. There were two men riding up front and in the back was a wooden coffin box—no flowers, no mourners following, just a single box coffin. The men riding up front tipped their hats at Momma as they slowed to stop for just a moment. Momma dropped her head and for the first and only time, a single tear rolled down her face. One of my sisters asked if she knew who was in the coffin. She only said, "You should always stop and pay respect when you see someone passing on their way home to glory."

The sheriff returned to our house a couple more times, asking Momma about Poppa's whereabouts, but her answer never wavered or changed. Eventually he stopped coming.

After several days past, Momma finally told us that our father was in the coffin that had passed by that day. She explained that was the only way he could get out of town alive.

I was a grown woman with children of my own before I saw my father again.

Hardie to Hartie

The only thing worse than wanting to leave the South and not being able to, was being told you had to leave. "You better be out of town before the sun goes down." That was a threat often made to Black men in the South by White men. You didn't have to do anything wrong in sunset towns, just being Black was enough. Black men were hated and feared by Whites more than anything else in the world. God forbid if you had done anything to upset or offend a White man by anything other than just your presence.

That was what happened with Poppa. He assaulted a White man. In addition to the sundown and sunset laws, there was also the Black Codes—laws that tried to get around freed Black people in the South by limiting where they could work and where they could travel for work. These laws limited the rights of Black people. We could sue and take other Black people to court, but not a white person. We could own property, marry, enter into legally binding contracts, but we didn't have the freedom to go and work wherever we wanted. So, were we truly free?

Hartie's father had run into trouble with this on a property he owned. Hartie and his brothers helped his father grow crops for sale. They had several different customers who bought from them regularly. There was a White man who had been buying from them for years. One year, another White man offered Hartie's father a contract if he would sell his crops to him only. Of course, that was a good deal for them. Hartie's father attempted to give the man who had been loyal the longest a chance to make the same or similar deal first. He went to the first guy and told him about the contract offer from the other man. The first guy got upset and asked if he could see the contract, as if Hartie's father might be lying. Hartie's father readily showed him the contract. The white man appeared to be a little stunned and shook up when he was handed the contract. He looked it over and then told Hartie's father to get the hell off his property. An hour or so later, the man came out to Hartie's property, complained about being insulted, and suggested that Hartie's father get out of town before the sun went down.

Leaving town meant leaving behind his farm, his business, and his family. This was a typical way Black men were driven out of business, and out of town. No one was willing to risk their lives or the lives of their families and loved ones, so most of the time they disappeared. I didn't know Hartie, and I certainly wasn't married to him during this time. This is something Hartie told me about after we were married. From what he told me, it was the White man who mysteriously disappeared, and was never seen or heard from again. No one ever knew what had happened to him. It was like he had just vanished. It was a short time after Hartie and his brothers went in different directions. Hartie went up North to look for work. He and his brothers worked up there for a time before returning to the South.

No sooner than Hartie's feet touched the ground in the South again, he was out looking for work. He went back to see the guy he worked for before he went up North. The guy had always thought Hartie was a good worker and was happy to hire him again. All Hartie had to do to start up again was fill out some paperwork. The guy reviewed Hartie's information to make sure everything was in order. After a couple of minutes, he turned to Hartie and asked him about the work he did in the North. Hartie explained to him why he had gone up North and what it was he did for work while he was there.

The man drew a long breath and then explained to Hartie that he was not going to be able to hire him after all. He told Hartie that it was illegal for him to leave the South and go work up North and that he or anyone else who hired him in the South would be breaking the law. He told Hartie that as soon as he gave someone his social security number on a job and they found out that he worked out of state, he would go to jail. That day he went from being Hardie Blake to Hartie Blake.

Last One Standing

I've never met a man like Hartie before. He was the same man from the day I met him to the day he died. I'm not saying that was good or bad. He was who he was. I was just a girl when Hartie came to visit his uncle, who was married to my mother. His uncle's name was Anthony Blake. I never could bring myself to call him my father. My father was smuggled out of the South in a coffin to escape the law when I was six years old. I never laid eyes on him again until I was a grown woman. When I ran into him again, I was married with children, and he was remarried with a whole new family. When I saw him, we looked at each other but neither of us acknowledged the other. I never saw him again. We lived in the same city and I was aware of his other family but that was as far as it went.

Hartie was divorced with four children when I met him. Hartie was twelve or thirteen years older than I was. Hartie told his uncle, "I'm gonna wait for as long as it takes because I'm gonna marry that girl." I was only sixteen years old at the time. Hadn't been that long since I had broken up with a boyfriend, and I didn't have any interest in another man. But for the fact that a voodoo woman was chasing after me, trying to put a spell on me so I would marry her horrible grandson. It was rumored that all she had to do was touch you and she could make you do anything she wanted. Her grandson had a crush on me, but I had no interest in him. I had become afraid to travel off our land. I hated the South and was willing to do anything to get out of it. I decided that I would marry the first man willing to marry me and take me out of the South. That person turned out to be Hartie Blake.

I didn't love Hartie and I think he was more attracted to me than he loved me. We liked each other well enough, but more importantly, we both wanted the same thing—to get out of the South. We skipped over the "love, honor, and cherish" and jumped right to "I do." And we did, but leaving the South didn't go exactly as we planned. We ended up sharecropping land for some old White man and living on his property. I hated every minute of every day of it. One day, while out in the field, I was chased by a blue race snake, or what we called a running snake. That was it for me. I told Hartie that I was never going back out in that field again, and I didn't.

Several years had gone by. Hartie and I had four daughters and my momma and the rest of my sisters had all moved up North. I was the first one who wanted to go and the last one stuck in the South. Hartie and I had our ups and downs right from the very beginning. He was as stubborn as I was. He was set in his ways something terrible. He did exactly as he promised, kept a roof over our heads, put food on the table, and clothes on the kids' backs. Nothing more, nothing less. Everything else having to do with running a household or caring for the kids was my job. I didn't mind up to a point. When I finally reached that point, I told Hartie I was leaving and going up North. He told me he wasn't going, and I could go without him if that was what I wanted. I called Momma and once she said that me and my girls could come live with her, I started packing. Hartie made a couple of comments here and there, not believing that I was going to leave. I just kept packing. When the day came to leave, I got the girls together and took off for the train. Before the train left, Hartie showed up, got on the train with us, and off we all went.

Up North, Hartie found work and started working immediately. The years went by quickly. We started out in a two-car garage behind my mother's house to a two-bedroom block apartment in an area they called The Lake, which was also known as Beck's Lake—a swamp surrounded by a garbage dump. As Blacks from the South continued to migrate up North for work on the railroad between Chicago and South Bend, many settled in South Bend. The city's land filled the area around the swamp and built low-income housing primarily for Black people. We took what was meant for bad and made the best of it. The Lake became a thriving Black community where everyone knew everyone, we all looked out for one another and kids grew up in a good, healthy, and safe environment. We didn't have no problem with White folks and they didn't have any problems with us.

We all lived like a community, shopped at the same stores, worked in the same places, our kids all went to the same schools, and everyone treated the children in the community as if they were all their own. Now to Hartie, he never showed a difference in one child from the other. Didn't matter if you were a girl or a boy, when he addressed kids, they were all "Heyyyy, boy" or "Heyyyy, boy" that. Even with his own, he called the boys either David or Fred, and the girls, Bessie or Gladys, or "you, you will do." The kids were used to it and never paid it no mind, but from time to time their little friends' feelings would get hurt. If you came to our house, Hartie didn't treat you any differently from one of his own.

On one occasion, the boys—Hardie Jr., David, and Fred—had one of their little friends over to the house. He was the

21

son of one of the community's preachers. I think it might have been the first time he was ever over to the house and didn't know Hartie as well as he should have. Hartie and I stayed up in the front of the house and the kids' rooms and everything was in the back of the house. Hartie loved watching Westerns and baseball on the television and anytime he watched one of those, he would get after the kids whenever they got too loud on the other end of the house and disturbed him. If they got too loud, he would stomp down to the other end of the house and raise the roof about the noise.

Afterward, the kids would quiet down for a while and then, little by little, get noisy all over again. Hartie went down and warned them several times before finally declaring that the next time he had to come down he was coming with the belt and was going to whoop everyone he saw. Now this was nothing new to the kids, it had happened many times before. They would push Hartie to the limit and when they heard him coming with the belt, they would all run and hide. Hartie didn't bother looking for any of them. He would get whichever ones he caught before they had a chance to hide. On this night after the final warning, he grabbed his belt and stomped down to the other end of the house. All the kids ran and hid except for the preacher's son. He didn't think he had to run or hide because he was not one of our kids. He didn't know Hartie very well. Hartie whooped him just as if he were one of his kids.

That little boy ran home crying and never came to our house again. I don't know if Hartie knew that the boy was not one of our kids or not. Later on, the kids told me that their daddy whooped their friend. When I told Hartie that he whooped the preacher's son, he told me, "When he in my house, he my son." That was who Hartie was from the day I met him to the day he died.

Next to the
Last Pea in the Dish

Walter was my next-to-last baby. He was a good baby, always on the quiet side, and seldom got into mischief or got the "devil in him," as we used to say. Walter suffered from asthma from the time he was a baby. Seems like most of his attacks would come in the evening or late in the night just as everyone was settled in their beds for the night. As a mother of a large family of kids, with their ways and personalities, over the years you get used to learning a little something unique and special about each one of them.

As the kids grew older, after a certain age, we allowed them to go out at night to friends, school activities, movies, and parties. Hartie worked late nights, so most of the time I would be the only one at home with the kids before midnight. I tried to be liberal and didn't have a real strict policy or curfew. During the week, it was before eleven and, no matter how late you stayed out, you went to school the next morning. The weekends, I was more flexible. I felt like I could be because I trusted my kids. Of course, that didn't stop me from worrying. After we moved to the west side, where we were the first Black family to live on our block, I was even more cautious. During most evenings, just by the activity in the house, I knew who was home and who was out. When I went to bed, I couldn't fall into a deep sleep until I knew all the kids were safe at home.

I would get into bed at night, but my ears would stay open, listening for the door to open and close. I'd listen for the sound of footsteps, whether they were fast-paced, slow and steady, or trying to tiptoe. I got to the point where I could tell who it was just by listening to their footsteps when they came in. Once I heard the last one come in, I would fall asleep. Walter and Robert were my last two who started to go out at night, but for the most part, they were always home early. Most of the time, their friends would come to our house. After so many, I was probably the most permissive with the two of them. Also, Walter was very responsible; never gave me one minute of trouble. He was also good at looking after his younger brother, Robert. They got along well together.

Because of Walter's good and responsible nature, I was stunned the day he came racing into the house crying. I was on the phone and as soon as I saw how upset he was, I instantly hung up to find out what was wrong. I was shocked when he told me that a teacher at school had kicked him. I had to make sure I was hearing correctly first. He told me that the teacher literally raised his foot and kicked him with it. Why the teacher did it didn't matter to me, but I asked Walter why anyway. He told me that the teacher accused him of doing something that he didn't do and when he protested that he didn't do it, the teacher grabbed him and kicked him. That was all I needed to hear. I got Walter and we immediately headed back up to the school.

Colfax School was just a short walk from our house. I didn't have any idea what I was going to say or do when I got to the school, but I could feel my temperature rising with each step I took. It was close to the end of the school day when this happened so school was out by the time we got there. Luckily, the school doors were still open, and we walked right in. Walter directed me to where his class was. I assumed I was going to come face to face with an older, angry-looking White man, rather than the one I found. This teacher was a much younger man than I imagined—he was not very tall, nor very angry-looking. He looked like he had just gotten out of school himself. I walked right up to his desk and introduced myself. I told him that my son, Walter, had come home and told me that he had been kicked in the backside by his teacher. I was trying to keep calm and give him a chance to assure me that there was some kind of mistake or misunderstanding.

However, that was not the case. He assured me that indeed Walter's account of what happened was accurate. I could feel the anger instantly welling up inside of me. Nervously, I looked around the room, just hoping to see something that would anchor me. I noticed he had this big tree-stump-looking rock on the corner of his desk. I guess it was a paperweight or something. I asked him, "What in the world made you think that you could raise your foot and kick my son with it?" He began to tell me that Walter did this and that, which Walter, standing right there at my side, denied to his face. I told him, "If you were talking about one of my other kids, even my youngest one, I might believe you, but not with this one. If he says he didn't do it, he didn't do it." I told him, "Your feet were made for walking. I had better not ever hear of you using it to kick another student again."

That's when he admitted to me that he had kicked another student all the way down the school stairs the other day. I wasn't sure if he was serious or if he was just trying to get my dandruff up with that comment. He sat there—behind his desk, not even bothering to get up when a lady entered the room—trying to justify why he felt like he could lift his foot and kick a child with it. My mind flooded with the memory of my last day of school when that White woman struck me across my back with that strap. I thought about my father having to escape the South in a coffin to avoid being lynched because he struck a White man in self-defense. Before I knew it, I had my hand on that rock on the corner of his desk. It seemed like I could smell my own blood in my nose. I was so mad; I could see myself bashing his head in with the rock.

Thank God I didn't go that far. When that rock slammed down on his desk, he immediately jumped up from his seat with terror in his eyes. He made some kind of statement about what would be all right with me.

I told him, "It's best to send mine home to me and their father and let us handle punishing them. It would be wrong of me to give him permission to hit one of mine, then change my mind and jump on him like a duck on water for doing it."

"No one else has been up to school outraged like you."

"I don't give a damn about what the other parents do or don't do. I had not ever catch you kicking one of mine or anyone else's again, is all I know."

Just about that time, the principal walked into the room and asked what all the commotion was about.

I asked him, "Is it school policy for teachers to kick students with their feet?"

The principal then made the mistake of telling me, "Calm down. There must be a misunderstanding." He wanted to explain to me that things were not always the way kids explained them.

"My son, Walter, came home and told me he had been kicked by a teacher, and his teacher confirmed that 'Yes' he did it. I let him know right away before he could go any further, that no one had better never kick one of mine again."

Suddenly, he suggested that either I calm down or he would call the police.

I told him, "I don't care who you call. None of mine had better never come home and tell me he had put his foot on them." I promised him that if that ever happened again, I would come up there and tear him from limb to limb. I repeated myself so I was sure I made myself clear to him.

The principal went as far as to suggest that I might consider removing my children from school if I had a problem with the way children were disciplined there.

"I am not going to remove my children from this school and as of this day, you have been served notice about how I expect you to treat my kids."

The principal tried one last pass at it. "Maybe we should speak with Mr. Blake in the future."

"You don't want my husband coming up here, trust me." That was all I had to say. I turned and left.

I was still shaking when I got outside. Walter followed closely behind me. I turned to Walter and told him that in the future I needed him to do the best he could to never get in trouble again. "I smelled my blood while I was talking to your teacher," I told him, "and I came very close to going to jail and leaving my kids without a mother." I looked at him. "Do you understand?"

His eyes grew wide, and he nodded yes.

We walked the rest of the way home in silence.

School Days

In 1938, I was fifteen years old and in my second year in high school at the only all-Black high school in Marked Tree, Arkansas. By this time, Momma was with her second husband, Anthony Blake. We had moved from Mississippi to his farm with him in Arkansas. Since my father had left her with hungry mouths to feed, what else was a woman to do? A lot of times in those days, divorces were not as common. People just did what they had to do. I'm not sure if Momma was legally divorced from my father or not. I knew that I had an aunt who had four husbands, and never divorced any of them when she left one or one left her. When she met another and decided to get married, she just did.

31

We got along with our new father fairly good most of the time. He was a tall man who took care of us and treated us well, but sometimes he could be a hard taskmaster. My siblings were all expected to do the work in the fields and whatever needed to be done. I'm not ashamed to say that I picked cotton, raised crops, and even chopped down trees and helped to pack them into bundles, ready to go to market.

Sometimes he would get after us about the way we did a certain job when we couldn't see no wrong with the work we had done. He would get the devil in him some days for no apparent reason. We would stand for it as best we could, but when we had enough, we had enough. On one particularly hard hot day, my sisters—Myra, Dolly—and I had all been working on cutting down some trees, hauling them, chopping them up, and bundling them when he got after us for something or another. He picked the wrong day—none of us were in the mood. When he grabbed ahold of my sister, the other two of us immediately went to work on him. Before he knew anything, we lit into him like June bugs. We each grabbed the first thing we laid hands on—a limb, a strap, whatever was readily available—and we beat him until Momma came and pulled us off him. He never bothered us much after that day.

I was still in school at the only school for Blacks. I had to walk two miles to get to school and two miles to get back home every day. When I would say things like that to my own kids later in life, they never seemed to understand what I was saying. To us, getting an education was a privilege, something that we would readily walk even a much further distance for. In my kids' days, not having the right clothes, having to catch a bus, or anything was a good reason to complain or not want to go to school, but I was blessed with good kids, no matter what the differences were between us. My teacher, Ms. Marie, was a short little, bright-skinned, nothing of a skinny woman, who favored the kids from town over those of us from the country. My sisters and I were not bad for looking, all were brown-skinned, had long hair down our backs, and all fully formed and shaped like women by the time we hit our teens. I can't say for sure but looks like to me both my looks and my being from the country were two things Ms. Marie just couldn't get past about me.

There were other girls in the class, some from the country just like me and others from the town who would tease and taunt me from time to time, saying things like "She thinks she cute because she got long hair" and stupid things like that. I would walk by, and they would say these things in Pig Latin: *"He-say (she,) hink-tay (think), hat-thay (that) he-say (she,), is-skay (is), ute-kay (cute), ause-kay (cause), he-say (she), ot-gay (got), ong-lay (long), air-hay (hair)."* This was some stupid, made-up language that occasionally the kids in town would use, thinking those of us from the country didn't know it for some reason. Of course, I knew and understood every word they would say about me. I never paid it no mind most of the time until one of the girls called me an *"Ong-lay (*long), aired-hay* (haired), *itch-bay* (bitch*)."* My first mind was to light right into her ass and tear her from limb to limb, but instead, I just said right back to her in Pig Latin, *"And ou-yae* (you) *is-skay* (is), *an ald-bay* (bald), *ead- hay* (head), *itch-bay* (bitch), *oo-tay* (too)."* It shocked the hell of 'em. Didn't particularly stop em,' just slowed em' down a bit and kept 'em from saying things to my face.

Ms. Marie was a strict disciplinarian who used to carry what gin belt, which was a strap that came off a cotton gin. It looked a lot like a razor strap used by barbers. If a student was to get out of line, she would either send them down to the principal's office—I forget his name now, but he was one of the tallest men I think I've ever seen in my life. Seems like she would particularly pick the students that she wanted to go after personally for some reason or another and use that gin belt on them. I knew that she didn't like me and I honestly tried as best I could to never give her reason to use that belt on me. I couldn't say or even think about what I might have done if she had struck me with that belt. Momma and Poppa would get after us a right smart when we deserved it, but they never allowed or permitted anyone else to raise a hand to us. Just the thought of having her hit me with that strap brought to mind the very reason why we lived in Marked Tree, to begin with. I could never forget how my father had to leave town in the dark of night behind the incident he had with that white man he nearly beat to death for striking him. I guess I kinda feared that Ms. Marie, me, that gin belt, and the inevitable would happen one day. It was always somewhere in the back of my mind that day would come.

And finally, it did.

She struck me with that damn gin belt. On this particular day, Viola, a girl I was friends with, and I were passing notes back and forth with another girl in class who didn't particularly like me. They kept the notes going back and forth until finally, I got a hold of one of them and found out that they were talking about me. I read the note and threw it back at Viola. They began throwing the notes and hitting me in the back of the head with them and laughing all the while. After a bit, Ms. Marie caught us just as I threw one of the notes back. She instantly rushed over and demanded that I pick up the paper off the floor. I attempted to explain to her what had taken place and that the girls were the ones who had started the whole mess, but she wasn't interested in hearing my side of the story. She just kept insisting that I pick the paper up. I protested that Viola and the other girl should have to pick up the paper as well as me, but she kept insisting that only I pick up the paper. I'm not sure why, but something just reared up inside of me and made me decide that either all three of us girls would pick up the paper or it would stay right where it was on the floor. I didn't know much about mincing or parsing words, so I didn't try to sugarcoat it when I told her I was not picking up the paper unless the other girls did.

That was all it took. She hauled off and swung that strap, hitting me right across my shoulder twice. I can't say I saw this color or that, I didn't see anything, nor could I remember anything at the moment. I jumped up and grabbed that gin belt from her, because the next thing I knew, I had it and instead of her beating me and me yelling out in pain, it was her. I went at that little ass of hers and tore her up. She squirmed and attempted to move away in this direction or that, but no matter which way she turned, I was on her like a duck on water. I must have given her a lick for every day of my life, every trial and tribulation, every hurt, anger, and disappointment I had ever known.

I thought I would whop her until I gave out, but about this time, the principal busted through the door. Some of the other kids in the classroom had run and got him. I looked up and he loomed in the door like the giant from Jack in the Beanstalk, with a scowl like a bulldog on his face, and the devil in his eyes. I'm not sure what I had in mind, but I headed straight for the door where he stood as fast as my feet would carry me. I'm not sure if I was planning on going around, over, or through him, but I was going to find out any second. Just as I got close, he reached out his long arms and I ducked down and went right between his legs. I raised up and he flipped over and went tumbling over my back. I had cleared the schoolyard by the time he hit the floor, I'm sure. I started running that day and it seemed like it was years before I finally stopped.

I had been running most of that year, long before this incident ever happened. In my school, there was a boy who had a crush on me. He was about as ugly as one person could be. He had this old grandmother who would come and walk him from school because a lot of time he would get teased and various things after school was out each day. The grandmother would come and walk him home because most people were afraid of her on account of it was widely believed that she practiced what I guess you would call black magic. Some would say she studied roots, charms, practiced voodoo, hoodoo, or whatever, but it was commonly accepted that she had powers. One of the most talked about stories about her involved an incident between her and another woman, who always hated her. This was over something that had started between the two of them way back, having something to do with one of them going with the other one's husband or man, or something like that—some of these things I forget all the particulars on now, but stemming from that they didn't have anything to do with one another.

To everyone's surprise, one day, this lady who studied the roots happened upon the other one and tapped her on the back. It was reported that when the other lady turned around, she greeted the "root" woman with a smile and kindness.

Later, she went to dinner at her home. A couple days later, she mysteriously was dead. Many folks say it was that touch on the shoulder that killed her. Folks always said that if the "root" woman could touch you she could make you do anything she wanted, including killing you.

I had had enough. I never returned to school again. I wanted to get as far away from that boy and his grandmother as I could. I begged and begged until Momma let me go stay with my sister, Myra, and her husband. They had just had their second baby and could use some help on their farm.

Sister Myra

I couldn't wait to get to my sister, Myra, and her husband's place. Couldn't wait to get away from all the craziness I had been living through the past couple of years. I regretted not finishing school. I had dreams of doing something with my life more than just marriage and farming, but as far as I could see, those dreams were gone now. My only thoughts now were getting as far from home as I could and making do the only way I knew how.

Myra was next to the oldest sister; she was married and had been with her husband for maybe three or four years. They had a little place they farmed and two babies: their son,

Meredith, was two years old, and a new baby, just a couple months old. Myra was glad to have me come because she and her husband were having a hard time keeping the fields and trying to take care of two babies, especially with the new baby in poor health. I started taking care of the babies and doing the chores around the house no sooner than I got there. Myra and her husband would go out each day and tend the fields from sunup to sundown and I would mind the children.

The oldest of the two, after a while, couldn't tell me from Myra. He used to follow me around and call me Momma. The youngest didn't seem to get any better, just lingered.

In those days, you didn't go to a doctor's office every time someone was sick like you can nowadays. We depended mostly on what cures and remedies we knew or used for ourselves. I began to grow more and more worried about the baby and told my sister that I didn't think the baby was going to make it if we couldn't get it seen by a doctor.

She would fret from time to time, but there wasn't much more than what we were doing that we could or knew to do. She just prayed that the baby would get better. I would spend most of the day just holding and rocking him. One day, while they were out in the field, and it seemed like I knew it was coming. The baby died. Died right there in my arms as I held it and rocked it. When my sister came in from the field, I had placed the baby back in the crib and told her that he had died. She didn't seem to fret much like she didn't believe me or something, or maybe she wasn't ready to accept it. She just continued to fix and prepare dinner. She went over and looked at the baby, but acted as if it was just sleeping. I told her again that the baby was dead. She just left him there as if he was sleeping for a while before it seemed as if she could understand and come to terms with it.

The next day, we took the baby out and buried it and that was it. I could see the pain and hurt in my sister's eyes, but life had to go on, she had to go on, we all had to go on and that's what we did. My aunt Anna, my momma's sister, used to always say, "The young will die and the old must die." I don't think Myra was ever the same from that day forward.

It wasn't too long before I decided to go back home to my mother's place. Momma worked as hard as any man and made extra money doing little odd jobs where and when she could. One of the things she did was work as what was called, a wet nurse. Many Black women back in the day would allow White women, who couldn't nurse their babies or didn't want to, some I suspect for vanity reasons, would bring their babies and let them nurse at the breast of a Black woman. This was not an uncommon practice, but not much discussed, because again for vanity reasons or maybe for the shame of it for the White women who did it. This was something that I had a hard time understanding because I always thought that White people hated Black people. I thought if they hated us so, then why would they bring their babies and allow them to suck a

Black woman's titty. This always puzzled me until one day I asked Momma, "How can they hate us like they do and yet bring their babies?" She said, "Because our milk is strong and nutritious." Then she looked at me in that "this is something you should never forget" way and said, "They don't hate us they fear us." She went on to say that all that they were and everything that they hoped to be was like a dream that was built on the backs of people like us.

From the moment we stepped off the slave ships, they turned a page in their history that they would never be able to come back from. The fear and dread of that very moment has kept them vigilant and on the clock, working day and night to hold us down, to control us, and to always be one step ahead. I thought, with all that fear and worry, no wonder the White man always seemed so stressed and the White woman so unhappy. From what I had heard, things were somewhat different in the North. It seemed like the White folks up North had a different mindset about Black people there than they did in the South. Didn't seem like they lived under the same constant terror as a Black man lived under day and night in the South. Freedom in the South had a different taste than freedom in the North. Again, whenever the subject of freedom would come up, Momma would say, "The only thing free in the South is the White man and Black woman."

Six Kids, Six Rakes

When the family moved into our new house on Oak Street, we finally had a full front and back yard on our property. We were the first Black family to move down to our end of the block. Further up the street, the neighborhood was a bit more mixed, but on our end of the street were just three White couples and Mr. Frank. Mr. Frank was an older White man, who looked like a dirty version of Alfred Hitchcock. He had a big beer gut and looked as if he wore the same dingy, yellow tee shirt and old pants every day. I suppose the tee shirt was probably white at some point in time. His lot had two small houses on it—the one he lived in and the one he rented out occasionally. Most of the time, the other house was vacant.

Mr. Frank would set outside on his front porch from around noon to late evening every day, drinking one beer after the other. You seldom saw him move further than his front porch. I don't think the other neighbors on the block had anything to do with him until I befriended him. Once I started to talk with him and would go over and sit on the porch with him some nights, one of the other neighbors would occasionally join us as well.

After I befriended Mr. Frank, the kids would offer to cut his grass for him in the summertime and shovel his walkway in the winter. He had a son who would visit him occasionally but did nothing to help take care of his father's property. Mr. Frank would pay the kids very well for shoveling his walkway and cutting his grass. I was determined that our yard was going to be kept as nice and clean as the other yards in the neighborhood. Especially with as many kids as we had and their friends who quickly made our house the meeting place where they gathered. I didn't mind, we never had any problems with any of the kids' little friends, and they were all very respectful. Since the yard was big, Hartie bought six rakes, so each of the kids had their own rake and they could all work together on keeping the yard up.

In the beginning, six kids, six rakes worked out fine. Dorine, Sharon, Jessie, and Forestine were the four oldest, and Walter and Robert were the two youngest. When it came to raking, the kids would split up the yard into areas and each took care of his area, then they all came together and bagged the leaves and put them out by the garbage. On occasion, the girls would pay the boys to do their part when they didn't want to rake leaves. Walter always seemed happier taking the girls' money than Robert. For Walter, raking the leaves was always an adventure. Sometimes, he would rake them all into a big pile and then jump off the roof balcony into them. I never approved of him doing that for fear that we would end up in the emergency room one day. Walter was always pretty obedient, maybe because he suffered with asthma for most of his younger years. He would wake Hartie and me up late in the night, unable to breath and we would have to rush him off to the emergency room. Maybe he thought he had to be good because it was always late in the night when he had problems with his asthma.

Robert Earl was the one I worried about if he would ever make it past his early childhood. He was the last pea on the dish, I would always say—born feet first, couldn't drink animal or human milk, instead he drank powder milk from a bottle until he was in kindergarten. He would fix his own bottle before he finally quit. Should have been a warning to me. I could not make him listen or do right to save my or his life. Walter couldn't help himself with his asthma, but when it came to Robert Earl, I don't know why, but he was so hardheaded. If he was told not to do it, he did it. We'd say don't touch it, he touched it. The nights with Walter in the emergency room were unavoidable, the trips to the emergency room with Robert Earl were because of a hard head. I remember telling him once if he didn't stop being so hardheaded, he was going to get Hartie and I suspected of child abuse one day.

But anyway, as the years went on, the girls, one by one, decided they were too old to rake leaves and the boys could do it. One year before Hartie left for work, he told me to tell the kids to rake the yard when they got home from school. He worked the second shift at the Allied factory plant from three o'clock to midnight, so he was gone by the time the kids got home from school, and they were in bed by the time he came in from work each night. I told them when they came home from school, and they started arguing about who was going to rake and who wasn't going to rake. In the end, nobody raked. In the morning, when Hartie went out in the daylight and saw that the yard had not been raked, he got to arguing and fussing. He always blamed me for being too easy on the kids. Again, he left instructions for the kids to rake the yard. Again, I told them, and again, they argued, and again, didn't rake the yard.

The next day, Hartie and I had the same argument over again, this time he had an ultimatum for the kids. I told them their daddy said if the yard wasn't raked by the time, he got home that night he was going to wake them up and make them rake in the middle of the night. That evening, I gave them the message from their daddy. The girls were still set on "If this one doesn't have to then I don't have to."

The only one willing to go out and rake was Walter. Robert Earl decided if the girls were not going to rake then he wasn't either. It was getting later in the fall and the weather was starting to get a little colder, so I really didn't want Walter to try to rake it all by himself because of his asthma. At the end of the night, everyone went to bed like it was nothing.

When Hartie came home later that night, he told me, "I see no one raked the leaves like I told them again." I didn't say anything. Hartie went into the kitchen, got something to eat, and watched TV for a while as he ate. As soon as he finished eating, I heard him walking through the house. I could hear from the bedroom, him stomping up the stairs to where the kids bedrooms were. As promised, he woke them all up and made all of them put on warm clothes and go out and rake the yard. We had a big light up on the back of the house that lit up the whole backyard at night. Hartie turned on the light and took a seat on the top step of the porch. He sat there and watched as the kids moved about, raking and complaining with one another about who was at fault. It was after two in the morning when the kids finally finished raking. It was also a school night. We never had that problem again.

The Dress

For years, my husband and I did whatever we had to do to take care of our family. Keeping a roof over our children's heads, and being able to keep food on the table, electricity, gas, and water turned on, along with making sure my family had clothes on their backs, meant everything to me. Trying to do this with thirteen children would not have been easy for the average White family, let alone a Black family in the Midwest. Yes, our struggles were not the mirror image of Blacks in the South who were still living with "No Coloreds" signs, but we certainly had our challenges in the North, too.

My husband sometimes worked more than two jobs—both day and night—to make ends meet. I did housekeeping.

I had three main homes I worked in. I cooked, cleaned, and did the laundry. The floors in the homes I kept outshined my own floors at home, but none of these families had all the feet traces over their floors throughout the day as I had traces over mine at home. I polished silverware and washed windows, things I seldom had the time or energy to do in my own home. They complained I made them do at home what I did for White people in their homes. Somethings I had to just take on the chin, because I was the one teaching my kids to always speak their minds and stand up for themselves. It never came back to kick me in my own ass, but it did challenge me from time to time.

Making sure my kids all completed high school was an unflappable goal of mine. Hartie only went through the third grade, and I went as far as my junior year of high school before dropping out. I would go to night school later in life and finally get my high school diploma. But anyway, I never demanded that my kids go outside the family looking for work and jobs. As long as they went to school and got their grades, Hartie and I would take care of everything else. With that understanding, it wasn't hard for my children to understand that with a family our size, clothes shopping would be done at rummage sales as opposed to store-bought. I explained to them that secondhand clothes I got from rummage sales were still new clothes to them. I meticulously washed anything I got from a rummage sale, and I always made sure that I

49

mended any tears and replaced missing buttons, or broken zippers before my kids ever wore anything I got from a rummage sale.

I did a right smart shopping for clothes in stores, too. I watched really closely for big sales. Usually, there were always the big "going-back-to-school sales," which was when I would do most of the shopping in stores for the year, and supplemented the rest here and there with rummage sale shopping. If my kids sought out other means to make their own money, I allowed it, if it didn't interfere with their schooling. That was rule number one. They took every advantage of that, that they could. During the winter they shoveled snow, and in the summer they raked leaves around the neighborhood to make extra money. After Hartie started hauling trash, the boys were always welcome to go out on the truck with him and help haul trash to make extra money. Even some of the girls wanted to do that as well, but Hartie didn't allow the girls to work on the truck. Hartie worked about as hard as any man I ever met, and I became particularly good at managing money. I used coupons, shopped sales, and bought in bulk whenever I could. Whenever there was a two-for-one sale on school supplies, I would get all the coupons I could and line the kids up in stores with coupons and we would buy enough supplies to last the whole school year.

There were times when people in the stores would complain about the amount of items I would buy when there was a limit, but I would point out that the limit was "per person," not per family. Even some of the store's workers would say things like, "Get ready, here she comes with her whole family again." I never paid much attention.

Eventually, the day would come when things started to get a bit easier. Hartie was making good money between his night job at the factory, and hauling trash. I had started writing "policy" on the side. We finally had a little bit of extra breathing room. I always made a point to pay bills in full and did very little buying things on credit. There came the day when with my A1 credit I decided to open a credit card at one of our main big department stores, Robertson's. On occasion, I would let one of the kids take the card and go down and shop without me. I always called the store first and let them know that I had given them permission to use the card. I seldom, if ever, had a problem with the store, until I did.

One day while shopping at Robertson's, I ran across a dress that I really liked and decided to treat myself. I hardly ever splurged like this for myself, but this dress caught my eye, was on sale, and I felt like I had to have it. It was a colorful print, the tag said it was a silk and polyester blend, which had been marked down several times.

I knew that the polyester blend meant that I could throw it in the washing machine, which made it even more of a good purchase for me. Even though I bought it right off the rack, I still washed it before I wore it. I put it in the kitchen sink and washed it by hand. To my horror, when I started to rinse it, all the colors had run one into the other. The dress was a faded mess. Just as I was standing there, holding up this mess of a dress, my sister, Dolly, called me. I was disgusted and told her I didn't have time to talk because I was on my way to return a dress to Robertson's. We worked far too hard for our money, and I was not about to throw it away like this. Dolly volunteered to go with me. I didn't bother attempting to dry the dress, I just stuffed it in a bag, dripping wet, and jumped in the car.

I stopped by and picked up Dolly on my way and off we went. When I got into the store, I went up to a sales clerk at one of the registers. I told her that I had bought a dress on sale, and I would like to return it. She was kind at first and asked me why I wanted to return it. I told her that when I washed it, all the colors ran and bled into each other. The sales clerk asked me if I could step aside and allow her to take care of the person behind me first. I didn't want to, but I did. As I waited, though, I began to get angrier and angrier. When she was finally finished with the other customer, the first thing she did was start to tell me about the store's policy regarding the return of sale items. I pulled out my receipt and gave it to her. She looked at it and began to explain to me that this item had been marked down so many times, that it was a final sale, and no return. She went on to suggest that maybe I didn't wash it properly. That was all I needed to hear. I opened the bag and pulled the dress out and held it in front of her face. It was still wet and started to drip all over the floor. The people standing behind me looked on in shock. Dolly got so embarrassed, she walked away. She knew I was about to tell this woman off. I raised my voice and told the sales clerk, "Oh, you are going to take this dress back today!" I told her I didn't need her or anyone else to tell me how I wash clothes. I told her, "I get paid for washing clothes. I suggest you get a manager and get one quick before I begin taking this store apart."

She got on the phone fast and called a manager. The manager came right away. He looked at the dress, then reached inside and looked at the label. He started repeating the same thing the sales clerk had started to tell me about maybe I didn't wash it properly. I told him that he has no idea how many years I have been washing clothes, or how many times people like his momma pay me to wash their clothes. Dolly came over and attempted to calm me down, fearing that the store would call the police on me. I didn't give a damn who they called. They were going to give me a new dress, or my money back. The manager asked me if I would step aside so the clerk could continue to help the people behind me. That's when I turned around and held the dress up so the people behind me could see it. I asked, "Does anyone want to shop at a store that sells shit like this?" I began to talk about how long I had been shopping at this store, and that I had their store credit card, and excellent credit with them. I told him that I would go to the newspaper, the Better Business Bureau, and bring all my children and picket in front of the store. I told him that I would do all of this and more until I got my money back.

That was all it took. The manager quickly decided that he would make an "exception" this time and return my money. He even offered that I could keep the dress if I liked, and he would still credit my store card. I asked him "What do you think I am going to do with this dress?" He offered me another dress of the same value for free if I just took the dress and left the store. I accepted his offer.

Time For a New Lawnmower

We moved from "The Lake" to the other side of town in the winter of 1964. We moved to 719 W. Oak Street, a four-bedroom, two-bathroom, upstairs, downstairs, and a basement. We had a full front and backyard, apple trees, grapevine, and a two-car garage at the edge of the backyard. Because the garage sat in the alley behind the house, it quickly became storage for everything Hartie had a mind to keep from hauling rubbish. Every now and then, Hartie would actually put an old car he and his friend, Kenny, wanted to work on in the garage, but it was mostly just for junk. Kenny was almost twice Hartie's age and had a piece of a storefront mechanic

55

shop that was closed about as often as it was opened. He worked more or less when he felt like it.

If you took your car to Kenny, you already knew that it might be there for a couple of months before you got it back. Whatever was wrong with your car when you took it to Kenny would still be wrong when you got it back months later. But he was a really friendly guy and a good mechanic when he set his mind to it. He and Hartie mostly worked on cars for entertainment. They would work several months through the hottest days of summer and the coldest days of winter fixing old broken-down cars. They would eventually get them running and sell them. After Hartie paid for parts and paid Kenny for helping him, he never made any money. It was just something to do mostly.

We still had our three oldest boys—Hardie Jr., David, and Fred—the six girls that followed them, and the two youngest boys, Walter, and the baby, Robert, me, and Hartie. The house on Oak Street was like going from a shoebox to a real house. Hartie and I had the single bedroom on the first floor of the house, and the kids were in the three bedrooms upstairs. Hartie Jr., fixed up a temporary bedroom down in the basement, but he would soon be going off to the military.

We were the first Black family to move into the neighborhood. I wasn't looking for nor did I plan to put up with any mess from either one of the two White households on either side of us. The two White ladies who lived in the houses on either side of me were sisters. One was open and friendly right away, the other was a bit more standoffish. As long as they were nice and respectful to me, we wouldn't have any problems. I didn't put it past either of them not to hesitate for one second before calling the police at the first hint of trouble or a problem. Hartie and I were determined to make sure that never happened.

Initially, we stayed to ourselves, trading hellos, good mornings, and that sort of thing in passing. Hartie was never the type to have too many words for White people. He was always polite but not one for engaging in long conversations with them. That was just his way. I could talk with anyone as long as they treated me right and we had something to talk about. Both Hartie and I had domestic work that we did for White people, so we knew how to deal with them. We made sure we explained to the kids how we wanted them to conduct themselves in the new neighborhood. This was the first time the kids lived this close to White people. The main things I was a stickler about were high school education, curfews, and keeping the yard up. I wanted to make sure that if my yard stood out in the neighborhood, it stood out for the right reasons.

For years, everything worked out fine. The kids, for the most part, did their part. I became close friends with one of the two ladies who stayed on either side of me. We even started a big garden in my yard together, which the kids called the "Snoop Sisters" garden. We also would take walks around the neighborhood some nights and keep an eye on what was going on around our block.

As will happen, we got older, and one by one the kids got older, got married, went to college, and were out on their own. Hartie and I finally found ourselves at home with just the two of us. From time to time, a grandchild, or other friend of the family would come by and cut the grass and do other little odds and ins for us.

Then one summer, Hartie decided he wanted to buy a new lawnmower and start cutting the grass again himself. Didn't make me no never mind, it was something to keep him busy. Over the years, the more things he would find to keep himself busy, the more nervous he would make me. One afternoon, Hartie told me he was going out to buy a new mower and off he went. A couple hours later, he came stomping through the house, complaining about buying a mower and someone stealing it off the back of his truck before he got home with it. I couldn't understand how something like that could have happened unless he stopped to put his numbers in, and someone took it then. He insisted that he left the store and came straight home but when he got out of the truck the mower was gone. The only thing I could tell him was to call the police and report it; go retrace his path home and see if he saw anyone with it.

After a couple of hours of complaining and accusing someone of stealing his lawnmower, Hartie decided he would go back and buy another one. Lord, help him, by the time he got home, he was complaining that the second lawnmower was stolen, too. I didn't know if he was losing his mind or what. It just wasn't logical that someone was jumping on and off his truck as he was driving, stealing his mower out of the back. Hartie was marching back and forth through the house, cussing everything and everybody. He was making me nervous with all that hollering. I got up to go outside to get away from all his hollering and the first thing I noticed when I looked at the truck was that the tailgate was down. Hartie was hollering about getting his gun and going back to the store to shoot somebody. He said that maybe the guy who sold him the mower was taking it back off the truck before he drove off.

Now both of us were hollering. I told him he was leaving the tailgate down on the truck and throwing lawnmowers out in the middle of the street as quickly as he could buy one. Of course, he asked me if I thought he was some kind of fool or something.

Bessie called just as things were starting to really get heated. She could hear Hartie yelling and raising the roof. She asked, "What is going on?"

I told her, "Hartie is buying lawnmowers and throwing them out in the street as soon as he drives off the store lot because he keeps leaving the tailgate open. Then by the time he gets home, he accuses someone of stealing them off the back of the truck."

Bessie has always been her daddy's daughter and she quickly told me, "Momma, stop yelling at my daddy and tell him I will come over tomorrow and go with him to buy a lawnmower and make sure it gets home with him."

The next day, Bessie came over and she and her daddy went and bought him a lawnmower. The third one in a week.

The Running Snake

Truth be told, I had not married for love, but to get out of the South. My two eldest sisters had already married and moved up North with their men and I was desperate to get out, too. We were all living on a farm with Momma and my stepfather, Anthony Blake, when his nephew, Hartie came to visit. I was sixteen, just about to turn seventeen at the time. It was early spring, and we were hard at work, tilling the land and getting it ready for planting crops when Hartie showed up.

Hartie was a tall light-skinned, good-looking man, but I didn't really pay that much mind. I had made up my mind when it came to getting together with a man, I was only interested in one that would get me out of the South. Hartie was twenty-seven, divorced, and had four children already. I had the mind and body of a woman but seemed like the thing that interested Hartie the most was my long hair and ability to work in the field as hard as any man. Didn't take him long before he let his interest in me be known. I let him know right off what my interest in him was, too. I don't remember if he ever asked me to marry him or not, it was more like a bargain. He promised he would take me up North and we got married. It was only after we got married that I learned more about who he was as a man.

The first disappointment was he didn't take me from the South but just from one part to the other. We spent the first few years bumping around from one part of the South to the other until we finally took up sharecropping. The year was 1945 or '46, I was just twenty years old, maybe twenty-one at the time, and we already had four daughters. We had already been here for about two years when one summer day changed everything for me.

It was about one of the hottest days in the field I had experienced, and I was already mad about something or another. We hadn't long started when I came face to face with a running snake. I'm sure they call it something else, but we called 'em running snakes because they would stand straight up on their tail and whop themselves around in a quick motion toward their target, but its real name is Blue Racer. It seemed to me, I was eyeing it, and it was eyeing me right back. For a hot minute, both of us were deciding what was next.

I guess my decision came first because before you know it, I took off. I ran through the field just as fast as my feet would carry me. I believe there might have been moments when my feet didn't even touch the ground. I was yelling and screaming like I was on fire or something, while the other fieldhands laughed and kept yelling something to me. I was running so hard and screaming so hard, I couldn't really make out what they were saying. Finally, I could make out that they were yelling, "Turn! Turn! Turn!" There was only field all around me. I couldn't figure out where to turn or why to turn. I had no idea these snakes could not turn, once they were on the move they could only go straight, so finally I turned and sure enough, it kept right on going past where I turned. After a moment it stopped, and I could see its head over the cotton, looking this way and that before going back down to the ground. I came out of the field that day and never went back again. I told Hartie that was it for me. We leave together, or I leave on my own. We left together.

Under the Sun, Below the Earth

I cannot honestly say I know what is above the clouds, or below earth. I was raised with Christian values, but none of my immediate family were staunch go-to-church people. My sister, Artisha, the one we called Sistah, got involved in the church after she was married. The rest of us went as we pleased. Momma never made no difference about it one way or the other. She did have a church that she was affiliated with, though. I did according to the Bible and took my children to church when they were young. I never forced them to go, but I encouraged them to go. Once they were of age, they made up their own mind. I can't say I believed in the Bible front to back, but I believed in most of it. I know in my life, I personally saw and witnessed things which are not in the Bible.

I have seen ghosts, spirits, and other things that ain't supposed to be real or happen with my own eyes. I had a problem with why God would make life and times so hard and difficult for some and so easy for others. Why would God allow for one man to enslave another? As far as I could tell, you couldn't find another race of people more faithful and serving God than Black people. So, a lot of things didn't match up in my mind the way they should. Hartie read the Bible almost every night, but never stepped foot inside a church. He could quote you chapter and verse of any scripture you named. I think the Bible was probably the only book he ever read. To this day, I don't know if it was for sport, or some other reason. He could argue with the best of them about how things in the Bible either matched up or didn't match up with things in the world. One of his favorite chapters was about Jonah being swallowed by the whale. Hartie would get so excited and laugh so hard when he talked about a fish big enough to swallow a man, and the man lived in the fish's belly for three days. I don't know if he believed it or not. On the other side, Hartie had a mean streak you would never know he had. If you got him on the right subject or the wrong day, he might tell you something that would make your hair stand on end. One would never know it, but he loathed White people.

Outwardly, he couldn't possibly have been more kind to them, but what he thought about them was far different. He used to say around the house, "The only good White man is a dead White man." I would constantly tell him don't say things like that to the kids. I couldn't see no point in talking like that. I had my feelings about White folks, too. I will never forget they were the reason my daddy had to run off and leave us when I was a little girl.

I understood Hartie, on the other hand, had seen and experienced the kinds of things I had only heard about. Hartie's granddaddy was a slave. Hartie had seen men lynched and hanging from trees. He saw Blacks' homes set on fire and they had to flee in the middle of the night with only the clothes on their backs. His own father was cheated and run out of business by a White man because he could read. It was these things and others that formed Hartie's feelings about White people. I would always try to stop Hartie from talking to the kids about most of these things. It was my goal to shield my kids from what I could, and at the same time instill a sense of pride in them. I made sure that they understood the threats and challenges they would face because they were Black. I just tried to instill it without the meanness that Hartie felt inside.

There was an incident that had me so scared and worried that I didn't know what to do. Hartie had started working at the Studebaker plant in South Bend. He worked on the second shift like he always did, so he could work on his garbage truck during the day. There was a White supervisor on the night shift who, for some reason, took a dislike to Hartie. Every night when Hartie showed up for work, that White man would stand there at the time clock and call Hartie a nigger. He did it night after night, and night after night Hartie would punch in and not say a word to the man. He would come home and raise the roof about it after work every night. I could tell it was eating him up alive inside, but I did not know what to tell him to do. Nothing that I suggested seemed to matter.

Finally, one night, Hartie came home and told me he had reached his breaking point. He told me that a man had called him a nigger for the last time. I asked him what he planned on doing and he told me straight out.

"I'm taking my gun to work tomorrow and if that son of a bitch calls me a nigger, I'm going to kill him right where he stands at the clock."

I did not know what to say. I begged him and begged him not to do it. I asked him, "What is supposed to become of me and your kids if you killed a man and went to jail?"

This is one of those times we all have where no matter what you believe or do not believe you pray to somebody or something as hard as you can.

I waited until the kids were all in bed sleeping. I tried to talk to Hartie again to see if I could talk him out of it. I called his brothers, Albert and Ludie, to see if they could talk to him.

His brother Ludie jumped in his car and drove over and he and Hartie talked for a good long while. I went into the bedroom while they talked and lay on my bed and prayed some more. After a while, Ludie left and Hartie came to bed.

"What did Ludie say? You still planning on killing that man?"

"Yes," and that was all he said. He rolled over in bed and I could hear him praying, too.

Remember, Hartie read the Bible just about every night before going to bed. After a while we just lay there until we fell to sleep. In the morning, Hartie was already gone before I woke up. I assumed he went out to do his regular trash route. I called my sister, Dolly, and told her everything. By the time we got off the phone, Hartie had come in. I fixed a pot of coffee, some eggs, and bacon. He ate without saying a word, but he seemed more relaxed, so I started doing my daily chores.

Later in the afternoon, as he was preparing to go to work, I got one last idea. I asked him to stay home and not go to work. "Just give it one more day and see how you feel after another day," I told him.

He agreed and stayed home. After he made up his mind that he was not going to work, he said he was going to his brother, Albert's, house. He was there most of the evening before he came back home. That night and the next morning went like the day before, we barely talked. Finally, the afternoon came, nearing time for him to leave for work.

"Do you think you should stay home another day?"

"There's only one way to fix the problem. Somebody had to go, either me or the White man."

I started praying again the moment he left. That was one of the longest days of my life. Every time the phone rang or someone came to the door, I jumped. I didn't know what I expected to hear or see, or what would happen by the end of the night. One hour after the next passed, my ears were tuned in for anything that sounded like a police siren.

As the hours passed and it got to be late in the evening and everything continued as it had on any other night, I started to feel a little relieved. Hartie said the White man always stood right by the time clock, calling him out of his name as soon as he went to clock in. Hours had passed since he would have clocked in, had something happened, I would have known by this time. The rest of the evening and night passed with no difference. Throughout the earlier part of the evening, I would watch and listen to the kids, happy that they knew nothing about what was going on, or about how their world could change in a heartbeat. I kept thinking about how something like this took my daddy away from us when I was a small girl.

As usual, right around midnight, I heard Hartie come through the front door of the house. I listened as he dropped his lunch box on the kitchen table. I heard his feet continue down the hall to the back of the house. Just like every other night, he turned the TV on and went and sat on the couch. I lay there in bed, wondering what had happened until I couldn't wait any longer. I jumped out of bed and went into the living room where he sat and asked him, "What happened?"

"The man didn't show up."

I thought, *God answers prayers after all.*

The following night when Hartie came home after work, things were a little different. He did everything he usually did except he didn't turn on the TV before he sat down. I sat up in bed and waited a minute to see if the TV would come on or not, it didn't. I got up and went into the living room and Hartie was just sitting on the couch, reading his Bible.

"Was the White man at work today?"

Hartie looked up and told me, "He's dead."

My heart sank to my feet. I thought I was gonna pass out. "Dead?"

"After he didn't show up for work, and no one heard anything from him, somebody went and found him dead."

I couldn't believe what I was hearing. "What happened?"

"Nobody knows for sure, maybe a heartache. They found him sitting at the kitchen table, dead." Hartie said he was told that it looked like he had sat down to eat and died right there at the table. He said they believed he had been dead for two days. "Thank God he spared me from having to kill that damn white cracker," was the last thing Hartie said about it before going back to reading his Bible.

As much as that was a relief and a blessing, I stopped short of calling it a miracle. You know the devil will try to play tricks on your mind sometimes, if you believe that kind of thing. In my mind, I kept thinking something about this sounded familiar to me.

Vi Was Her Name

Hartie woke me up, asking, "Who is that in the kitchen?" "Hartie, I'm in bed with you. How do I know who is in the kitchen?" I went on to say, "It must be one of the kids."

"Smells like somebody is making coffee. None of the kids drink coffee."

That's when it hit me. I jumped out of bed, threw on my duster, and hurried out of the bedroom. I told Hartie I just as well get up and get his breakfast started. Hartie always had a habit of waking up a little before he had to get up, pestering me with whatever was on his mind. Most was stuff about hauling trash, who paid him, who owed him money, and who he was going to cut off. That was the typical way our mornings started.

There she was, roaming through my kitchen cabinets. She had two kettles on the stove. Hartie hated instant coffee, so I had several old kettles I used to brew his coffee. The woman in my kitchen had one kettle for coffee and another for tea boiling on the stove. Vi was a White woman I found sitting on the curb, crying the evening before. In the evening, Lois Lynn—the White woman who lived in the house next to me—and I would take little strolls around the neighborhood after we finished fussing about in our garden or sitting on the porch talking. While we were on our walk the night before we came up on a lady sitting on the curb crying. Lois was content to keep walking as if she didn't see anything.

I said, "I wonder what's wrong with her?"

Lois instantly said, "It isn't any of our business," and kept walking. The main reason we went on these walks, if the truth be told, was to keep tabs on what was going on in the neighborhood.

The kids painted a sign attached to a scarecrow that read: "The Snoop Sister's Garden," because of our nightly vigils around the neighborhood. My family was the first Black family to move down on the end of the street in our neighborhood. As a matter of fact, we were the only Black family in our entire block of homes for a good long while. When we moved in, Lois stayed on one side and her sister, Millie, lived in the house on the other side of us. Lois was friendly right off, but her sister and her sister's husband took a while before they warmed up to us. In the beginning, Millie and her husband didn't pay us no mind, and we didn't pay them any mind. As time went on, Lois and I started talking more and more over the fence and then eventually visiting on one another's porch. I think Millie began to feel left out, and slowly started to come around.

Millie was more concerned with what to call me than getting to know me first. I remember her asking one day, "What do you prefer to be called?" I wasn't tracking where she was going when she asked the question, so she went on to ask, "Do you prefer Colored, Negro, or Black?"

"You can call me Louise, Mrs. Lousie, or Mrs. Black, or you don't have to call me anything." That took care of that. We never revisited that subject. But back to what I was talking about.

Our neighborhood was not the kind of neighborhood where you would expect to find a White woman or a Black woman sitting on the curb crying. She looked to be around Lois and my age and was well-dressed. I was as curious as I was concerned. It surprised me a little that Lois didn't seem to have any concern for one of her own kind. The most she offered was to call the police once we got back home.

I asked the woman if she was all right or if she needed help. Before I knew anything, she was up on her feet, hugging me, thanking me for my concern. That caught me off guard. She had a thick accent, which made it hard to understand everything she was saying. I understood something about being abandoned and left all alone on the street with nowhere to go. Vi was from England. She had been corresponding for months with a man who convinced her to come to America with the promise of marriage. Two weeks after getting here, she discovered he was already married. They had a fight and he dumped her and all her luggage on the street and drove away. She knew no one else in America and had nowhere to go. I looked at Lois and she looked away.

Lois lived in a four-bedroom home just as big as mine, with just her and her husband. I thought she could offer this woman a place to stay for at least a night. In hindsight, when I thought about it, I didn't know what came over me or why I thought either of us should bring this woman home with us. Maybe Lois had the right idea about calling the police and letting them handle it. Before I knew it, I was helping the stranger from England collect her things and I brought her home with me. Even as we walked, I didn't have any idea what I was going to do with this woman. As soon as we got near our houses, Lois instantly went inside and closed her door. Vi and I sat outside my house and talked for a long while. We called the police. They came out and listened to her story, but told her there was nothing they could do. They advised her to seek shelter at a hotel or a shelter for women. All she had was a few dollars to her name, her suitcases, and a few other personal belongings.

It was already getting late, and I couldn't bring myself to turn her out into the streets, so I told her she could stay for the night in my basement. My basement was finished with a refrigerator and bed. My oldest sons had converted it for themselves before they got married and moved out. It was a convenient place where she could stay for the night. I did find her an interesting woman. I didn't know much about England, so the things she talked about, how she talked about things, and the way she phrased things was interesting. One by one, as my kids realized that this strange lady was going to be staying in our basement for the night, they gave me looks like they were wondering if I had gone crazy or not. As many strays as they brought home over the years, I didn't know why this was such a surprise to them.

Now here she was, early in the morning, in my kitchen, rattling pots and pans, trying to make something called a scone. She asked if I had any marmalade or sweet gravy to put on scones. All I could think about was how I was going to tell Hartie about this woman in his house. Mind you, Hartie had some very hard opinions about White people. In public, on his job, or as far as anyone outside of our house knew, Hartie didn't have an unkind thought in his head about anyone. But "under his roof," I had to constantly get behind him about some of the things he would say in front of the kids. Granted, just as I had, in his life, he had witnessed and personally experienced some unforgivable things at the hands of White people. He had to change his name from Hardie to Hartie behind some White man laws that were aimed at limiting and keeping track of Black people's whereabouts back in the day. That is another story to be told at another time.

Hartie walked into the kitchen to find Vi and me sitting at the kitchen table, having a cup of coffee. It was not totally uncommon for me to have a White woman in my home, so Hartie just said "Good morning, ma'am" as he was accustomed to doing when greeting a White woman. I fixed him a plate and poured him a cup of coffee. He picked them up and took them to the other end of the house where he always sat and watched television.

Vi and I continued talking at the table. The kids started to come down and file through the kitchen on their way out for school. I passed out lunch money as they filed by, not missing the lingering and questioning looks on their faces. Vi had little pleasant comments to make to each one as well. They were very respectful and greeted her with smiles and friendly gestures. After everyone was gone and we finished breakfast, Vi instantly got up and started in on the dishes. I told her she didn't have to, but she insisted. When she finished, she went back down into the basement. I went down on the other end of the house where Hartie was sitting. From where he sat, he could see Vi as she went down the stairs into the basement.

Hartie casually asked me, "Who is that lady, and what she is doing down in the basement?" I told him she was washing

77

some clothes. He was already reaching for his hat when he asked, "You renting out your washer and dryer now?" I didn't say a word, I just let him keep going.

Later on, after a lot of telephone calls, even to England, promising she would pay for it, Vi asked if she could stay a couple more days. I said yes. Now I had no choice but to tell Hartie. He hit the roof when I told him. His exact words were, "You done lost your goddamn mind, woman? I'm working day and night to feed and keep a roof over all these kids' heads and everybody they drag up in here and now you bring a White woman for me to take care of, too? Let her own kind take care of her." Like I always did, I told him to stop all that foolish talking.

His last word on the subject before he stormed out again was, "I ain't taking care of no White woman in my house!"

I knew he would cuss, holler, and act a fool but would settle down by the time he came back. What I didn't know was that a couple of days would turn into weeks. The kids and their friends had gotten used to Vi quick enough. They either ignored her or humored and joked with her. She was full of stories and interesting little sayings. She helped around the house with dishes, mopping floors, and cleaning. She attempted to cook several dishes but that was where everybody pumped the brakes. I wouldn't dare serve anything she cooked to Hartie. Hartie stopped using his and my bathroom downstairs and started bathing exclusively upstairs

78

in the kids' bathroom. He kept saying that he wasn't taking any chances on having a White woman making accusations about him and get him hung. Sometimes, I would laugh at some of the things that would come out of his mouth, but I knew they came from a history of witnessing some horrible things in his lifetime.

Vi wasn't a bad-looking woman at all and she had a nice figure. I got the idea that I would play matchmaker and introduce her to our insurance agent who came around once a month to collect insurance policy money. He had a reputation for being a lady's man around the neighborhood. It was rumored that he had fathered a couple of children that lived on his routes. I introduced the two of them, and they hit it off right away, going out three or four times a week. Some nights she didn't come back at all. I thought Hartie would be happy about that, but then he said he didn't want a White woman teaching his daughters bad habits. I couldn't win for losing with that man. Hal, the insurance agent, thought she was the neatest thing he had ever met. He was very taken with her being English.

I was just hoping that things would continue going in the direction they were going before neighborhood gossip about Hal's outside kids got to Vi's ears. You couldn't have convinced Vi that she hadn't found Jesus in a jug no how.

One day, Hartie came home and told me, "That's it. You have to get rid of that woman." He told me that on his job, people were starting to say he had a Black woman and a White woman both living in the same house. Ordinarily, Hartie was not the type to concern himself with gossip, but when it came to him and a White woman, he didn't take that lightly. He also said the kids were starting to act like they had a White housekeeper, and he wasn't crazy about that either. "She needs to go before she turns this whole damn house crazy." He told me that if I didn't want to tell her he would tell her. He said he would take her and drop her off at the welfare office and that would be a lot better than what that White guy did for her.

Just goes to show how God steps in and has the final say when you try to do the right thing. Later that evening, Vi came back and announced that she and Hal were getting married and that she would be leaving the next morning for Niagara Falls. I was very happy for her. Hartie said, "That damn fool; she done jumped out the skillet and into the frying pan. That Hal liable to put insurance on her then push her ass over in the river." I just looked at him.

I heard from Vi once or twice a year over the next few years. After about five years had passed, she and Hal showed up for a visit. They had moved to Florida and were still happily together.

We Called Them Haints

Once my baby Robert Earl was in school all day, it was easier to get out and about to do my running without having my baby under foot. I could spend a whole day just grocery shopping and going to rummage sales. The things it took to run a household with as many kids as we had were all the things Hartie hated doing. In his mind, working, putting food on the table, paying bills, and keeping a roof over our heads was his only job. Hauling me or the kids around was not his job in his mind. If he ever had to take me to the store, he would fuss and complain there and back. It was the same with the kids when it would come to him having to drop them off at places. The kids didn't like it much either, because he had a rule about driving other people's kids around—he wouldn't. "I got enough responsibility keeping mine alive, I ain't going to be responsible for no one else." He talked a right smart just to hear himself, I think. Hartie, his brother, Albert, and his brother, Ludie, could argue with their own shadows if it stayed behind them long enough.

Over the years I learned to block out most of his cussing and fussing. When he got going, and I got tired of listening, I would go down to the other end of the house and let him cuss and fuss by himself, and that's exactly what he would do. Sometimes, he would follow me from room to room. He used to drive me nuts when he would go out one door cussing and a few minutes later, in he would come through another door still cussing. Didn't matter what he was fussing about. One minute it would be this and then it would be about something the kids left on the lawn, or they needed to cut the grass, anything to keep a fuss up. The "in one door and out the other" was something he did regularly that drove me crazy. I used to say to myself, "He going to make me chop his head off one day." We had three doors to the house: front, back, and a side door. He would wait until it either rained or snowed, and then, just as I started mopping, he would come marching in one door, and then out another one, tracking up my floor as I was mopping. Some days he would be out all morning, but as soon as I put mop to floor, in he would come, tracking up my clean floors. No point in me saying anything because I knew it would only lead to fussing and me wanting to chop his head off, so I lived with it.

Hartie had a truck for hauling rubbish and a car, and I had a car. After the kids were all off to school, I would start the day by doing a couple of loads of laundry. By this time, the phone would start ringing. It would usually be Dolly, my sister, Mrs. Harris, or Ms. Bernice, two old ladies I used to drive around. Ms. Bernice and Mrs. Harris were in their late sixties and neither of them drove. Ms. Bernice was a Polish woman who lived up on Chapin Street. She had a storefront rummage shop, but she bought more merchandise, and gave away more merchandise than she ever sold. She had stuff piled from floor to ceiling, with just one narrow little path you could walk through. She lived in a room in the back, which was as full as the front of her shop. She was about four feet tall, walked like she had crippling arthritis, never washed and combed her hair, and always wore the same flowered dress. She rarely smiled, but on occasion she would say something funny and laugh at herself. She had a quick sense of humor for an old lady. She was perfectly at home, living up on Chapin Street, right in the middle of "The Block," a block well known for gambling, pimps, and prostitution. She didn't bother anybody, and nobody bothered her.

Mrs. Harris was a Black woman, also small in stature, who lived on my street about three blocks up the way. I don't think she was ever a young woman or a nice woman. The kids in the neighborhood called her Mrs. Crabby because she never spoke to them, just sat on her porch scowling and mean-mugging everyone who walked past her house. Her husband was like a ghost. He could be sitting in the room with you, and you wouldn't even know he was there. She had him so henpecked that he didn't say a word unless she told him to. Hartie used to haul her trash for her until she finally tore her ass with him. When he came home fussing and called her an old bitch, I knew that was it for him.

I would take her to doctor appointments and grocery shopping. Some days she would get in my car and not open her mouth coming or going. She didn't like this, or she didn't like that and didn't like kids. Anytime my baby, Robert Earl, was with me she would be mad. She liked making the kids mad when she would call by calling me out of my name when one of them answered the phone. She would say, "Is that old heffa home?" or little things like that. One day my daughter Sharon answered the phone and cussed her out. As soon as she told me, I knew exactly who she had talked to without having to ask. She was livid, but it stopped her from talking like that to the kids. She also had a bad habit of opening things in the store like cookies, grapes, or gum and stuffing it in her purse. I figured one day they would catch her and that would be that.

One morning, just after dropping Ms. Bernice off at her place, I was driving up Chapin Street toward Washington

Street to go home. Just as I got to the light at the corner of Chapin and Washington, I slowed the car down as I came to the light. Someone was walking across the street, but all I saw was a body walking with no head. Up around the collar where there should have been a neck and head, was just an empty collar with what looked like a blood stain around it. The hair at the back of my head stood straight up on my neck. Everything sped up instantly from that moment on. I don't know what color the light at the intersection was, I don't know if there were any other cars on the street. All I know is I hit the gas pedal and pressed it all the way to the floor. It was almost a straight shot from there to home, maybe four blocks. I don't remember looking to the left or right of me or for any other traffic, or anything else.

All I can remember after that moment was running into my front door over and over until Hartie finally opened it. I don't know what happened to my keys to the house, or if I didn't attempt to use them. I would run into the door, get knocked back, and then run into it again. I don't think I thought to try the doorknob, I just kept running into it. When Hartie pulled the door open, I ran directly into him.

He stared at me like I had lost my mind and asked, "Louise, what the hell is wrong with you?"

I was completely out of breath. I struggled to get the words out of my mouth to tell him what I had just seen. When I was finally able to tell him about the headless man, I was surprised by his response.

85

"Louise, why you acting a fool like that? That "Haint" been walking around Washington Street without a head for years."

Haints were what we called ghosts ever since I was a little girl. Hartie told me some story about the two guys who had gotten into a car crash around that intersection. One of them lost his head in the accident and supposedly had been walking around down there looking for it ever since. Little comfort did that bring me.

Later when Hartie went outside, he found my car door still open, the engine running, my purse on the front seat, and one of my shoes in the driveway. It was a long time before I ever drove alone down Washington Street. I never saw the headless man again.

Who Was
Louise Owens-Blake

I can't imagine Mom as a baby, little girl, or teenager; in my mind, she was always the woman she was when I was born. Although there is clear evidence that she experienced all those stages of life, I envisioned her as always having been a woman, wife, and mother. I know she was once a little girl because she shared stories about her childhood growing up in the South, including the games she played after school and the chores she had to do. It was surprising to learn that many of the games we played as children were the same ones she enjoyed as a young girl.

87

She was one of nine children born to Dell Owens and Lou Creatia Patton, with six sisters and three brothers. She was born on the farm where she spent her childhood. In 1923, when she was born, it was common practice for a midwife to assist with deliveries, which was the only option available to Black families at that time.

Over the years, there has been confusion about Mom's actual date of birth. She was born on February 3, 1923, but her official birth date was recorded as June 3, 1923, which was the date the midwife recorded.

As a young girl, she attended a small all-Black school and never experienced a school with White teachers or students. On most days after school, she and her siblings worked on the family farm, helping to harvest crops and pick cotton. Once she was old enough, she learned to plow the field using a horse and plow. At the age of six, her father was driven out of town following an altercation with a white man, and she would not see him again until she was a grown woman.

Her mother soon remarried a man named Anthony Blake, who turned out to be somewhat of a tyrant. She and her sisters never really got along with him. He made their lives miserable, especially when it came to working in the fields. Nothing they did ever seemed to meet his standards, and he constantly berated them. One day, things reached a breaking point when he started beating one of the sisters. Mom and another sister grabbed the first thing they laid hands on and began hitting him in defense. After that, the incident was never spoken of again. Her mother never acknowledged it, and Anthony Blake never laid a hand on any of them again.

From that day forward, it became a mission for Mom and her sisters to find any means possible to escape the farm and the South. My mom desperately wanted to finish high school, but a combination of factors made that unlikely. In addition to a stepfather she disliked, there was a voodoo woman who chased her around, trying to put a spell on her. The voodoo woman wanted to make her marry her ugly grandson by casting a spell with a single touch. However, that only made Mom a fast runner.

The last straw came one day in class when her teacher struck her across the back with a leather strap. This triggered a flashback to her experiences with her stepfather and sisters. Before she realized what she was doing, she grabbed the teacher and the strap and began beating her back. She said, "I turned her every which way but loose." The principal, an imposing figure, rushed into the room upon hearing the commotion. Mom recalled that she took one look at him as he rushed towards her, bent down and ran straight between his legs to escape. She was in the eleventh grade, and that day marked the end of her high school experience.

Shortly after that, she went to live with and help one of her older sisters, who had just given birth to her second child. She took care of her sister's babies while her sister and brother-in-law tended to their farm. After several long weeks, she returned to her mother and stepfather's farm, more determined than ever to leave the South one day. That's when her stepfather's nephew, Hardie Blake, came for a visit. He was a tall, handsome man, almost fifteen years older than she was, with an ex-wife and four children. She had promised herself that she would marry the first man who was willing to take her out of the South. Although she was only seventeen, she felt like she had lived the life of a woman twice her age. She wasn't sure if she was ready for marriage, but she knew she was ready to leave the South. The marriage would be based more on an arrangement than on a courtship.

Five years later, with a husband and four daughters, she was still living in the South. She and Hardie had only managed to move from one part of the South to another. They worked as sharecroppers, laboring in the fields from sunup to sundown nearly every day. She was beginning to think she would never get out of the South until one day she encountered a snake in the field. That was the last straw. She declared she would rather live in the gutter up North than stay in the South. She gave Hardie an ultimatum: she was moving up North with or without him. They eventually moved up North, and their first home was a garage instead of a gutter. Hardie quickly found work, and just as quickly, they transitioned from living in a garage to their first proper home.

Mom and Dad did not see eye to eye on hardly anything;

their marriage was not a warm and fuzzy romantic union. However, they shared a common motivation, determination, and abiding respect for one another. The marriage endured serious bumps and rough spots over the years, but they maintained an unwavering commitment to each other and to raising their family. Having been raised by a stepfather, Mom made a vow to herself that she would never live under a man who wasn't her children's father. She would stay in the marriage for the sake of her children until hell froze over or until the last child was out of the nest. For their sixtieth wedding anniversary, my brothers and sisters wanted our parents to renew their vows, but both respectfully declined.

Over the years of their marriage, Mom persevered through tumultuous and gut-wrenching times. She stood shoulder to shoulder with Dad, cleaning homes and offices, hauling garbage, and raising thirteen children. As time passed and we grew older, Mom began pursuing some of her other passions in life. She became a voice for her local precinct before moving on to serve the larger community through a pilot program called "Model Cities," which helped provide housing for low-income families. In 1972, she finally achieved a lifelong goal: she returned to school and earned her high school diploma.

Over the years, I never once heard Mom express a desire for material things. When asked what she would like for her birthday, Christmas, or any other occasion, her constant answer was, "I already have everything I want." It wasn't until she was in her eighties when pushed to the limit to answer the question, "What would you like if you could have anything in the world?" that she finally took a moment for deep soul-searching. After a while, she said, "I would love to be treated like a queen for a day." She got her wish. *Omebo* magazine, which is dedicated to helping people fulfill and live their dreams, along with other family members, provided her with a luxury, all-expense-paid weekend. She and a guest of her choosing were whisked away by limo to Chicago, where they stayed in a luxury suite, were pampered like never before, and enjoyed theater and dining fit for a queen.

Blake Family Reunion

Louise-isms

Little Pearls of Wisdom Mom Dropped Regularly

Whites vs. Blacks: *"They don't hate you; they fear you. White women wouldn't bring their babies to nurse on a Black woman's breast if they hated her."*

Burning bridges: *"Never tell a person to kiss your ass until you're in front of them."*

Having children after having thirteen: *"I wouldn't take a million dollars for any one of the ones I have and wouldn't give a dime for another one."*

Loaning money: *"Never lend more money than you can afford to give away."*

Free vs. pay for: *"I just assume pay for it because free cost too much."*

Liars: *"If you will lie, you will steal. If you will steal, you will kill."*

More on lies: *"If you are going to tell a lie, stick with it to the end."*

Secrets: *"If you have a secret and you can't keep it, don't give it to me and expect me to keep it."*

A vow to self: *"I had a stepfather growing up and made a vow to myself that I would never put a man who was not my children's father over my children."*

Punishing children: *"I would rather punish my children myself at home rather than have a police officer kill them out in the streets."*

'Til death do we part: *"If a man tells you he can't live without you, chances are he don't want to die without you either. First chance you get, you better run because I guarantee you, he will kill you and himself."*

Modesty: *"Keep your drawers up and your dress down."*

About the Author

Born in 1960 as the youngest of seventeen children in South Bend, Indiana, Blake Roberts grew up in a household where activism, religion, politics, and entertainment were regular topics of discussion. His passion for storytelling emerged early, as he wrote, directed, and staged his first play in the fourth grade. By high school, he had expanded his creative pursuits to include acting.

Encouraged by his talents, Blake continued honing his craft in college, joining the drama department and performing in university productions before becoming part of The New Stage Production Repertory Company. After college, his role as a writer and director flourished. He co-wrote, co-directed, and co-produced the production *Soul Shadows* in 1982, which debuted on the biggest main stage in South Bend.

In 1984, Blake relocated to Los Angeles, where he worked at Lorimar and Warner Bros. Studios while continuing to write, direct, and produce. His original play *Clippings* in 1996 became his first short film, garnering nominations at the LA Short Film Festival. He also co-wrote and directed the off-Broadway play *Faith Under Fire*, based on the life of publicist LaJoyce Brookshire, performed at the National Theater of Harlem.

In 2007, Blake began writing *ExtraOrdinary*, a collection of short stories inspired by life, in collaboration with his beloved mother. This project, a deeply personal work, has been both a source of inspiration and emotional growth over the years.

Made in the USA
Las Vegas, NV
12 November 2024

11659550R00062